SECRETS TO CULTIVATE A POSITIVE MINDSET

PRACTICAL STRATEGIES FOR ACHIEVING SUCCESS

DR. JAGADEESH PILLAI

Made with ♥ on the Notion Press Platform
www.notionpress.com

|| Dedicated to all wisdom seekers around the world ||

ꙮ

Contents

Contents

PRAYER

"Om Bhadram Karnebbhih Shrunuyaama DevaahBhadram Pashyemaakshabhiryajatraah Sthirairangaistushtuvaamsastanoobhih Vyashema Devahitam YadaayuhSwasti Na Indro VridhashravaahSwasti Nah Pooshaa VishwavedaahSwasti Nastaarkshyo ArishtanemihSwasti No Brihaspatir DadhaatuOm Shantih, Shantih, Shantih"

The literal meaning of this mantra is: OM. O Gods! Let us hear auspicious words from our ears. O reverent Gods! Let us behold propitious visions from our eyes, let our organs and body be stable, healthy, and strong. Let us do that which is pleasing to the gods in the life span allotted to us. May Indra, inscribed in the scriptures, bring us fortune! May Pushan, the knower of the world, grant us prosperity! May Trakshya, who vanquishes enemies, bestow us with blessings! May Brihaspati bring us success!
OM Peace, Peace, Peace.

About The Author

Dr. Jagadeesh Pillai is a renowned Guinness World Record holder, writer, and researcher hailing from Varanasi, also known as the abode of Lord Shiva. With a Ph.D. in Vedic Science and a range of creative ideas and achievements, he is a true polymath. He is the author of more than 100 books including Research Publications. Although his roots can be traced back to Kerala, the people of Varanasi hold him in high regard and affectionately consider him one of their own.

Dr. Pillai has achieved four Guinness World Records in the following subjects:

"Script to Screen" - In this record, Dr. Pillai produced and directed an animation film within the shortest time possible, breaking the previous record set by Canadians. He has also received numerous national and international awards and recognitions for this achievement.

Longest Line of Postcards - For this record, Dr. Pillai created a line of 16,300 postcards on the occasion of the 163rd anniversary of Indian Postal Day. The event also included a questionnaire about the Indian flag.

Largest Poster Awareness Campaign - Dr. Pillai designed an awareness campaign on the subject of "Beti Bachao - Beti Padhao" (Save the Girl Child - Educate the Girl Child) to achieve this record.

Largest Envelope - In tribute to the Indian Prime Minister's

"Make in India" initiative, Dr. Pillai created a 4000 square meter envelope using waste paper to achieve this record.

Attempted - **70000 Candles on a 210 kg Cake** - To celebrate the 70th Indian Independence Day, Dr. Pillai attempted to light 70,000 candles on a 210 kg cake, which was recorded in World Records India.

Attempted - **Documentary on Dhamek Stupa of Sarnath in 17 Languages** - Dr. Pillai attempted to create a documentary on the Dhamek Stupa of Sarnath, dubbing it in 17 different languages. The result of this attempt is currently awaiting confirmation from the Guinness World Records.

Dr. Pillai is skilled in teaching the Bhagavad Gita, a Hindu scripture, and is popular among young people. He has helped many young people improve their lives through his motivational teachings.

In addition to teaching, he has composed and sung numerous Sanskrit Bhajans and patriotic songs.

He has also written and directed several short films and documentaries for awareness campaigns, and has volunteered with the police in both UP and Kerala to spread awareness about various issues through videos and photography.

Incredibly, he has produced and directed over 100 documentaries about the city of Varanasi, all on his own.

He has also helped and guided more than 25 boys and girls to achieve world records through creative and innovative methods. He is a multifaceted person who uses his intellect and the blessings given to him by God to excel in various areas. He is both a teacher and a student, always learning and teaching, and is able to master any subject he comes across.

He is a selfless social activist and motivational speaker who has overcome struggles and failures to become a successful and enthusiastic individual with a rich life experience.

In addition to his work with the Bhagavad Gita, he is also an efficient Tarot card reader, Astro-Vastu consultant, and a talented singer and composer. He has sung the entire Ram Charita Manas and Bhagavad Gita in his own compositions, and has sung the phrase "Lokah Samastha Sukhino Bhavantu" in 50 different languages. He is currently working on a detailed and scientific study of Vedas, Upanishads, Puranas, and the Bhagavad Gita. He has also composed and sung the Hanuman Chalisa and Gayatri Mantra in 108 and 1008 different compositions, respectively.

Awards - Four Times Guinness World Records, Winner of Mahatma Gandhi Vishwa Shanti Puraskar, Mahatma Gandhi Global Peace Ambassador, Kashi Ratna Award, Dr. APJ Abdul Kalam Motivational Person of the Year 2017, Mother Teresa Award, Indira Gandhi Priyadarshini Award, Bharat Vikas Ratna Award, Udyog Ratna Award, Vigyan Prasar Award, Poorvanchal Ratn Samman.

PREFACE

The preface of the book "**Secrets to Cultivate a Positive Mindset: Practical Strategies for Achieving Success**" serves as an introduction to the main themes and ideas that will be explored throughout the book.

This book begins by highlighting the importance of a positive mindset for achieving success in all areas of life. It explains how a positive mindset can help individuals overcome obstacles, achieve their goals, and lead a happier and more fulfilling life.

The book is designed to provide readers with practical strategies for cultivating a positive mindset. It covers a range of topics, including understanding the power of positive thinking, identifying and setting goals, overcoming negative thoughts, developing a positive attitude, practicing visualization, developing positive habits, practicing self-compassion, increasing motivation, understanding the power of gratitude, mindful communication and taking action.

This book is not only for people who are already successful, but also for people who are looking to achieve success in different areas of their lives. The book is written in a way that is easy to understand, and the strategies discussed can be applied by anyone looking to improve their mindset and achieve their goals.

The book "Secrets to Cultivate a Positive Mindset: Practical Strategies for Achieving Success" provides an overview of the main themes and ideas that will be explored throughout the book. It explains that the book is designed to provide readers with practical strategies for cultivating a positive mindset and achieving success in all areas of life, and it's written in a way that is easy to understand and can be applied by anyone.

I

Understanding the Power of Positive Thinking

Practical Strategies for Achieving Success". This chapter aims to help readers understand the power of positive thinking and its role in achieving success in various aspects of life.

Positive thinking is the practice of focusing on the positive aspects of life, rather than dwelling on the negative. It is about looking for the good in every situation, and seeing the potential for growth and opportunities in challenges. Positive thinking is not just about being happy or optimistic, it is about looking for the best in ourselves and others, and believing that we can achieve our goals.

Positive thinking has been shown to have numerous benefits for our mental and physical health, as well as our overall well-being. Research has shown that people who practice positive thinking tend to have lower levels of stress, depression and anxiety, and are more resilient in the face of adversity. Positive thinking also has been linked to improved physical health, better sleep, and a stronger immune system.

Positive thinking is also a key component in achieving success. When we believe in ourselves, and have a positive attitude, we are more likely to take action and make things happen. Positive thinking helps us to see opportunities where others might see obstacles, and to keep going when things get tough. It also helps us to stay motivated and focused on our goals.

One of the best ways to develop positive thinking is through the practice of gratitude. When we take time to appreciate the good things in our lives, we are more likely to focus on the positive and to be more optimistic. This can be as simple as keeping a gratitude journal, where we write down things we are thankful for, or practicing mindfulness, where we focus on the present moment.

Another important aspect of positive thinking is visualization. Visualization is the practice of picturing yourself achieving your goals in your mind. When we visualize ourselves succeeding, we are more likely to believe it is possible and to take the necessary actions to make it happen.

"Understanding the Power of Positive Thinking - Exploring the power of positive thinking and its role in success" is an important chapter that highlights the significance of positive thinking in our lives. Positive thinking not only improves our mental and physical health but also helps us to achieve our goals and aspirations. It is a powerful tool that can help us to overcome challenges and to create the life we want. By understanding the power of positive thinking, we can start to cultivate a positive mindset and work towards achieving success in all areas of our lives.

"A positive mindset is the key to unlocking your full potential."

৪ত

II

Identifying Your Goals - Learning to Identify and set Achievable Goals

This chapter aims to help readers understand the importance of identifying and setting goals, and how it is related to positive thinking and success.

Setting goals is essential for achieving success, as it provides direction and motivation. When we have a clear idea of what we want to achieve, we are more likely to take action and make things happen. Goals also give us a sense of purpose and help us to stay focused on what is important.

The first step in setting goals is to identify what is important to you. This can be done by reflecting on your values, interests, and passions. Identifying what is truly important to you will help to ensure that your goals are meaningful and motivating.

Once you have identified what is important to you, the next step is to set specific, measurable, and achievable goals. Specific goals are those that are clear and defined, such as "I want to increase my income by 20% in the next year." Measurable goals are those that can be quantified, such as "I want to lose 10 pounds in the next six months." Achievable goals are those that are realistic and within your reach, such as "I want to save $10,000 for a down payment on a house in the next two years."

When setting goals, it is also important to consider the SMART criteria. This stands for Specific, Measurable, Achievable, Relevant, and Time-bound. This will help you to set goals that are clear, measurable and achievable, while also being relevant to your overall aspirations and having a specific time frame in which you want to achieve it.

Another important aspect of goal-setting is to break down big goals into smaller, more manageable steps. This makes it easier to focus on one step at a time and to track progress. It also helps to reduce the feeling of overwhelm that can come from tackling a big goal all at once.

"Identifying Your Goals - Learning to identify and set achievable goals" is an important chapter that highlights the significance of setting goals and how it relates to positive thinking and success. Setting specific, measurable and achievable goals, and breaking them down into smaller steps, can help you to stay motivated and focused on what is important. By learning to identify and set goals, you can start to create a clear path towards achieving success in all areas of your life.

"Your mindset determines your reality."

III

Overcoming Negative Thoughts - Recognizing and Changing Negative Thought Patterns

Negative thoughts can be defined as thoughts that are harmful, unproductive, or self-defeating. They can take many forms, such as self-doubt, worry, fear, and anger. Negative thoughts can be triggered by a variety of factors, such as stress, past experiences, or even physical health. They can be detrimental to our well-being, and can lead to negative emotions, such as sadness, anxiety, and depression.

It is important to recognize and acknowledge negative

thoughts, but it is also important to learn how to change them. One way to do this is through the practice of cognitive reframing. This is the process of identifying negative thoughts and then reframing them in a more positive or constructive way. For example, instead of thinking "I will never be able to achieve my goal," you can reframe the thought to "I may face challenges, but I will find a way to overcome them and achieve my goal."

Another way to overcome negative thoughts is through the practice of mindfulness. Mindfulness is the practice of paying attention to the present moment, without judgment. It can help to reduce the impact of negative thoughts by providing a different perspective. When we are mindful, we are less likely to be caught up in our thoughts and more likely to be able to step back and see things objectively.

Another helpful strategy is to challenge negative thoughts. This is done by questioning the validity of the thought, looking for evidence to support or disprove it, and considering different perspectives. When we challenge negative thoughts, we are less likely to be swayed by them, and more likely to see things in a more balanced way.

"Overcoming Negative Thoughts - Recognizing and changing negative thought patterns" is an important chapter that highlights the impact of negative thoughts on our lives and how to overcome them. The chapter emphasizes on the importance of recognizing, acknowledging and changing negative thoughts in order to cultivate a positive mindset. By learning how to overcome negative thoughts, we can start to create a more positive and constructive perspective, which can lead to greater well-being and success.

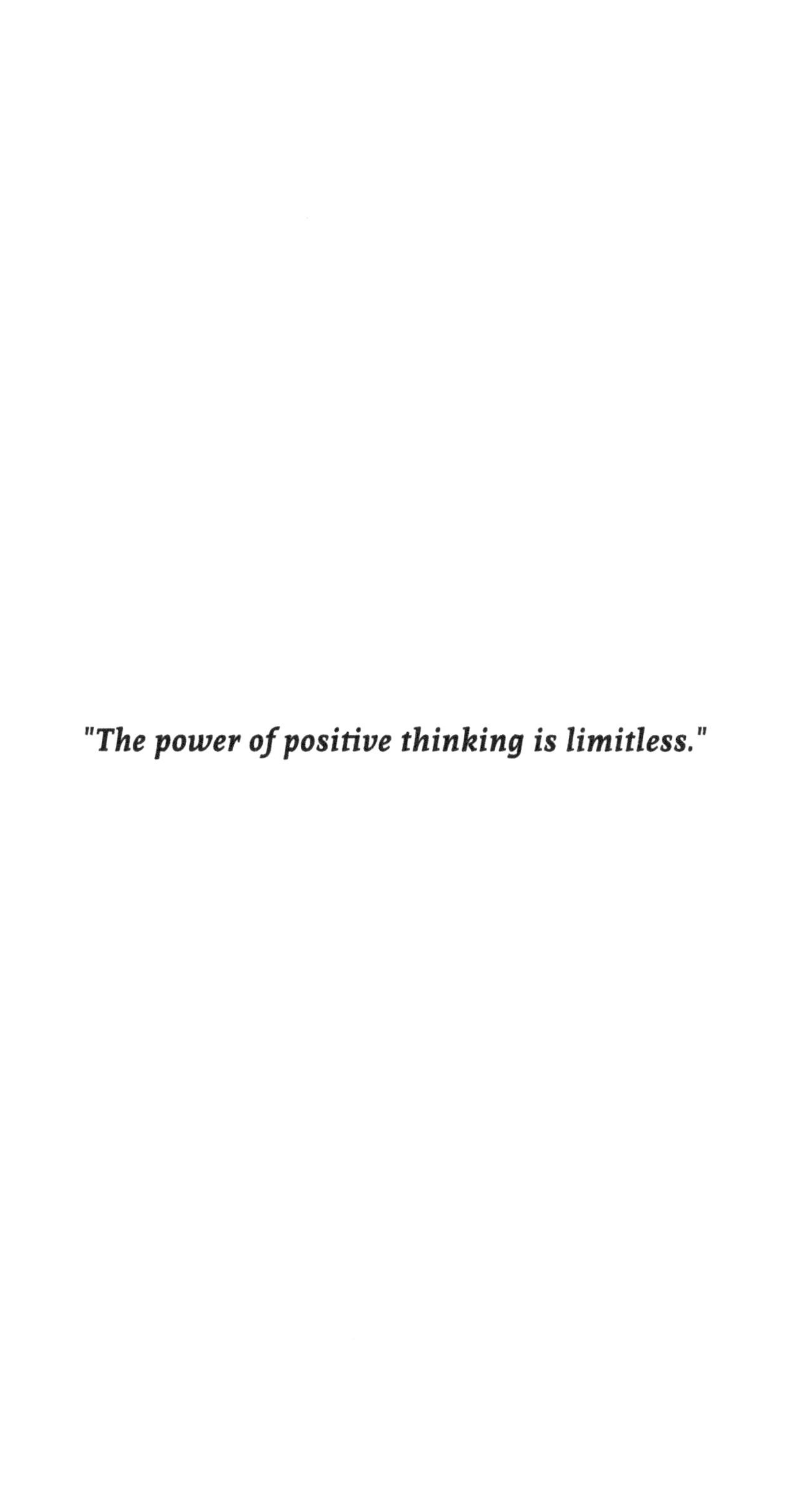

"The power of positive thinking is limitless."

IV

Developing a Positive Attitude - Strategies for Creating a Positive Outlook

A positive attitude is a mindset that is characterized by optimism, hope, and resilience. It is the belief that good things can happen and that challenges can be overcome. People with a positive attitude tend to have better physical and mental health, greater resilience, and a more fulfilling life.

One of the most effective ways to develop a positive attitude is through the practice of gratitude. Gratitude is the practice of being thankful for what we have, rather than focusing on what we lack. When we are grateful, we tend to see the positive in life, and we are less likely to be affected by negative thoughts and emotions.

Another way to develop a positive attitude is through the practice of positive affirmations. Positive affirmations are statements that we repeat to ourselves, in order to change our mindset. They can be used to overcome negative thoughts and to reinforce positive beliefs. For example, repeating the affirmation "I am worthy of love and happiness" can help to overcome feelings of self-doubt and insecurity.

Another strategy for developing a positive attitude is to surround yourself with positive people. Positive people tend to have a contagious energy and can help to lift our mood and outlook. By spending time with positive people, we are more likely to be exposed to their positive attitude and energy, which can help to change our own mindset.

"Developing a Positive Attitude - Strategies for creating a positive outlook" is an important chapter that highlights the importance of having a positive attitude and how to develop one. The chapter emphasizes on the importance of gratitude, positive affirmations and surrounding oneself with positive people. By developing a positive attitude, we can start to see the world in a more positive light, which can lead to greater well-being and success.

"Positive thinking is the foundation of success."

ꕥ

V

Practicing Visualization - Learning the Power of Visualization and How to Use It

Visualization is the process of creating mental images of what we want to achieve. It is a powerful tool that can help us to focus on our goals, overcome obstacles, and achieve success. By visualizing what we want to achieve, we can create a more vivid and realistic picture of it in our minds, and this can help to increase our motivation, focus, and confidence.

One of the most effective ways to use visualization is to create a clear and specific image of what we want to achieve. This can be done by writing down our goals, creating a vision board, or using other visual aids. By creating a clear and specific image, we can make our goals more tangible, and this can help to increase our motivation and focus.

Another way to use visualization is to use it as a form of mental rehearsal. This can be done by visualizing ourselves achieving our goals, and by imagining the different steps that we need to take to achieve them. By mentally rehearsing what we want to achieve, we can increase our confidence and reduce our fears and doubts.

Another way to use visualization is to create a positive visualization. Positive visualization is the process of visualizing positive outcomes and it can help to reduce negative thoughts and emotions. When we visualize positive outcomes, we are less likely to be affected by negative thoughts and more likely to see the positive in life.

"Practicing Visualization - Learning the power of visualization and how to use it" is an important chapter that highlights the power of visualization and how to use it to achieve one's goals. The chapter emphasizes on the importance of creating a clear and specific image of the goal, using visualization as a form of mental rehearsal and creating positive visualization to reduce negative thoughts and emotions. By using visualization, one can increase their motivation, focus, confidence, and reduce fears and doubts, which can lead to greater success in achieving one's goals.

80 03

"A positive attitude is the compass that guides you towards your goals."

ꟈ

VI

Developing Positive Habits - Learning How to Develop Positive Habits to Foster Success

Habits are actions that we perform regularly and automatically, without much thought. Positive habits are those that help us to achieve our goals, improve our well-being, and move us closer to success. Negative habits, on the other hand, can hold us back and prevent us from achieving our goals.

One of the most effective ways to develop positive habits is to start small. This means starting with small, manageable changes that are easy to implement and maintain. For example, instead of trying to change everything at once, start by making one small change, like drinking a glass of water every morning. Once this habit is established, you can then move on to making other small changes.

Another way to develop positive habits is to use a habit tracker. A habit tracker is a tool that can be used to track progress and keep you accountable. It can be as simple as a piece of paper or an app on your phone. By tracking your progress, you can see how far you've come and stay motivated to continue.

Another way to develop positive habits is to find a role model or accountability partner. A role model is someone who has already achieved the habit you want to develop and can give you guidance and inspiration. An accountability partner is someone who will hold you accountable and support you in your journey to develop a new habit.

"Developing Positive Habits - Learning how to develop positive habits to foster success" is an important chapter that highlights the importance of developing positive habits and how to do so. The chapter emphasizes on the importance of starting small, using a habit tracker, and finding a role model or accountability partner. By developing positive habits, one can improve their well-being, achieve their goals and move closer to success.

"Visualization is the bridge between your dreams and reality."

ᘓ

VII

Practicing Self-Compassion - Understanding the Importance of Self-Compassion

Self-compassion is the act of being kind and understanding towards oneself, especially during difficult times. It involves treating oneself with the same kindness, care, and understanding that one would offer to a good friend. Self-compassion is different from self-esteem, which is based on the belief that one is good or worthy. Self-compassion is based on the understanding that everyone makes mistakes and has difficult times and that it is normal to be imperfect.

One of the most effective ways to practice self-compassion

is to talk to oneself in a kind and understanding way. When facing difficult times, instead of being harsh and critical towards oneself, one should talk to oneself with kindness and understanding. This can be done by using positive affirmations and by reminding oneself that it is normal to make mistakes and that everyone goes through difficult times.

Another way to practice self-compassion is to practice mindfulness. Mindfulness is the act of being present in the moment and accepting things as they are. By practicing mindfulness, one can be more aware of one's thoughts and feelings and can respond to them with kindness and understanding.

Another way to practice self-compassion is to practice self-care. Self-care is the act of taking care of oneself and it can include activities such as exercise, meditation, and spending time with friends and family. By practicing self-care, one can improve one's physical and mental well-being and can better cope with difficult times.

"Practicing Self-Compassion - Understanding the importance of self-compassion" is an important chapter that highlights the importance of self-compassion and how to practice it. The chapter emphasizes on the importance of talking to oneself in a kind and understanding way, practicing mindfulness, and practicing self-care. By practicing self-compassion, one can improve their well-being, better cope with difficult times, and foster success.

"Positive habits lead to positive outcomes."

ꕥ

VIII

Increasing Your Motivation - Tips for Increasing Motivation and Taking Action

This chapter aims to help readers understand the importance of motivation and how to increase it in order to take action and achieve their goals.

Motivation is the driving force that propels us to take action towards our goals. Without motivation, it can be difficult to start or stick to a task, making it harder to achieve success. However, there are many ways to increase motivation and take action towards achieving one's goals.

One of the most effective ways to increase motivation is to set clear and specific goals. By setting clear and specific goals, one can focus their efforts on achieving them, making it more likely to happen. When setting goals, it is important to make them SMART (Specific, Measurable, Attainable, Relevant and Time-bound).

Another way to increase motivation is to find meaning and purpose in one's goals. When one finds meaning and purpose in their goals, it becomes more meaningful and fulfilling, making it more likely for one to take action and achieve them.

Another way to increase motivation is to break down large goals into smaller, more manageable tasks. By breaking down large goals into smaller tasks, one can focus on one task at a time, making it less daunting and more achievable.

Another way to increase motivation is to reward oneself for achieving small milestones along the way. This can provide a sense of accomplishment and encourage one to continue working towards their goals.

"Increasing Your Motivation - Tips for increasing motivation and taking action" is an important chapter that highlights the importance of motivation and how to increase it. The chapter emphasizes on the importance of setting clear and specific goals, finding meaning and purpose in one's goals, breaking down large goals into smaller tasks and rewarding oneself for achieving small milestones. By increasing motivation, one can take action towards achieving their goals and foster success.

"Self-compassion is the fuel for personal growth."

ꝏ

IX

Understanding the Power of Gratitude - Learning the Power of Gratitude and How to Cultivate It

This chapter aims to help readers understand the power of gratitude and how to cultivate it in order to foster success.

Gratitude is the feeling of appreciation and thankfulness for the things, people, and experiences in one's life. It is the act of recognizing and valuing the good things in one's life. Research has shown that gratitude can have a positive impact on one's mental and physical well-being. It can improve one's mood, reduce stress, and increase overall happiness.

One of the most effective ways to cultivate gratitude is to keep a gratitude journal. A gratitude journal is a place where one can write down things they are grateful for on a daily basis. This can include anything from small things such as a beautiful sunset to larger things such as a supportive family. By regularly writing in a gratitude journal, one can focus on the positive aspects of their life, and increase their overall well-being.

Another way to cultivate gratitude is to practice mindfulness. Mindfulness is the act of being present in the moment and accepting things as they are. By practicing mindfulness, one can be more aware of the things they have to be grateful for in their life.

Another way to cultivate gratitude is to share it with others. By sharing gratitude with others, one can increase the positive feelings associated with it and strengthen relationships with others.

Another way to cultivate gratitude is to practice acts of kindness. By performing small acts of kindness, one can feel a sense of satisfaction and fulfillment, which can lead to feelings of gratitude.

"Understanding the Power of Gratitude - Learning the power of gratitude and how to cultivate it" is an important chapter that highlights the power of gratitude and how to cultivate it. The chapter emphasizes the importance of keeping a gratitude journal, practicing mindfulness, sharing gratitude with others, and practicing acts of kindness. By cultivating gratitude, one can improve their well-being, foster success, and strengthen relationships with others.

"Motivation is the spark that ignites the fire of success."

ꕥ

X

Mindful Communication - Exploring the Power of Mindful Communication

This chapter aims to help readers understand the power of mindful communication and how to use it to foster success.

Mindful communication is the practice of being present, fully engaged and aware of one's thoughts, feelings, and actions when communicating with others. It involves paying attention to the words, tone, and body language used in communication, as well as understanding and responding to the emotions and perspectives of others.

One of the benefits of mindful communication is that it can help to improve the quality of relationships. By being present and fully engaged in the conversation, one can build trust and understanding with others, leading to stronger and more meaningful relationships.

Another benefit of mindful communication is that it can help to reduce conflicts and misunderstandings. By paying attention to the emotions and perspectives of others, one can respond in a way that is more likely to be heard and understood, reducing the likelihood of conflicts.

Another benefit of mindful communication is that it can help to increase empathy and compassion. By understanding and responding to the emotions and perspectives of others, one can develop a deeper understanding and appreciation for the experiences of others, leading to increased empathy and compassion.

Another benefit of mindful communication is that it can help to improve one's ability to listen actively. By being fully engaged and aware in a conversation, one can improve their ability to listen actively and understand the perspective of others.

"Mindful Communication - Exploring the power of mindful communication" is an important chapter that highlights the power of mindful communication and how to use it. The chapter emphasizes the importance of being present, fully engaged, and aware of one's thoughts, feelings, and actions when communicating with others. By practicing mindful communication, one can improve the quality of relationships, reduce conflicts and misunderstandings, increase empathy and compassion and improve one's ability to listen actively. These skills can lead to better communication, understanding, and ultimately foster success.

"Gratitude unlocks the door to a limitless future."

ꕥ

XI

Taking Action - Developing an Action Plan for Success and Implementation

This chapter aims to help readers develop an action plan for achieving success, and provides strategies for implementation.

The first step in developing an action plan is to identify specific, measurable and achievable goals. These goals should align with one's values and purpose, and should be challenging, but attainable. Once the goals are set, it is important to create a plan of action that outlines the specific steps that need to be taken to achieve them.

The next step is to develop a strategy for implementation. This includes setting a schedule, creating a timeline, and identifying the resources that will be needed to achieve the goals. It is also important to establish a system of accountability, whether it is through regular check-ins with a mentor, coach or accountability partner, or through setting up reminders and tracking progress.

Another important strategy is to focus on taking small, consistent actions towards one's goal. This approach can help to build momentum, increase motivation and reduce the feeling of overwhelm.

It's also important to be flexible, as things may not always go as planned. Be ready to adjust your plan and adapt to changes as needed.

Another strategy for implementation is to find a support system. This can be friends, family, or a community of like-minded individuals who share similar goals and can provide support, encouragement and accountability.

"Taking Action - Developing an action plan for success and implementation" is an important chapter that provides readers with the strategies they need to turn their goals into reality. The chapter emphasizes the importance of setting specific, measurable, and achievable goals, creating a plan of action, focusing on taking small, consistent actions, being flexible, and finding a support system. By following these strategies, readers can develop an action plan for achieving success and increase their chances of implementation and achieving their goals.

Other Books Of The Author

1. The Moments When I Met God
2. Kashiyile Theertha Pathangal
3. GURU GYAN VANI
4. Abhiprerak Gita
5. ASSI SE JAIN GHAT TAK
6. Hopelessness of Arjuna
7. The Soul and It's True Nature
8. Sense of Action (Karma)
9. Action through Wisdom
10. Action through Wisdom
11. THEORY AND PRACTICAL OF EVERY ACTION
12. LOGICAL UNDERSTANDING OF THE SUPREME
13. THE IMPERISHABLE SUPREME
14. Yatra Nishadraj se Hanuman Ghat Tak
15. Yatra Karnatak Ghat se Raja Ghat Tak
16. Yatra Pandey Ghat se Prayagraj Ghat Tak
17. Yatra Ranjendra Prasad Ghat se Dattatreya Ghat Tak
18. YaatraSindhiya Ghat se Gwaliar Ghat Tak
19. Yatra Mangala Gauri Ghat se Hanuman Gadhi Ghat Tak
20. Yatra Gaay Ghat Se Nishad Ghat Tak
21. MAA GANGA, GHATEN EVM UTSAV
22. Ganga Arti Dev Deepavali evam Any Utsav
23. Potentials of Digitalized India
24. VEDIC CONSCIOUSNESS
25. A Brief Introduction to Vedic Science
26. Kashi ke Barah Jyotirling
27. IMPACT OF MOTIVATION
28. Let's have a Milky Way Journey
29. Color Therapy in a Nutshell

30. Rigveda in a Nutshell
31. Yajurveda in a Nutshell
32. Samveda in a Nutshell
33. Atharva Veda in a Nutshell
34. Ayushman Bhava - Ayurveda
35. Srimad Bhagavad Gita and Upanishad Connection
36. Srimad Bhagavad Gita - an attempt to summarize each chapter.
37. Facts and Impact of Nakshatra
38. Astro Gems - NAVARATNA
39. Ekadashi - A Concise Overview
40. A Concise View of Hanuman Chalisa
41. Inspirational Gita
42. Nakshatraranyam
43. Summary of 18 Mahapuranas
44. Synopsis of 18 Upa Puranas
45. Rigvediya Upanishads
46. Shukla Yajurvediya Upanishads
47. Krishna Yajurvediya Upanishads
48. Samavediya Upanishads
49. Atharvavediya Upanishads
50. The Seven Great Sages
51. From Rocket Scientist to President Dr. APJ Abdul Kalam
52. The Visionary's Voice - Quotes of Dr. APJ Abdul Kalam
53. The Wisdom of Swami Vivekananda: Insights and Inspiration from a Legendary Spiritual Teacher
54. Ayurvedic Remedies from the Garden
55. Sages and Seers
56. Rising Strong – Motivational Stories of Women
57. Beyond Flames -Mystery stories of Funeral Ghat Manikarnika
58. The Origins of Tulsi: A Look at the Mythological Roots of the Plant"

59. The Holistic Cow: A Look at the Physical, Spiritual, and Cultural Importance of Cows in India
60. Arts of Healing
61. Exploring the Divine
62. Understanding Five Elements
63. The Etymology of Ram
64. Symbols of India
65. Voice of Change (About Speeches of Great Men)
66. She Speaks (About Speeches of Great Women)
67. Patriotism on Celluloid – Brief About Patriotic Films
68. The Music of Motivation: A Brief Guide to Inspirational Film Songs
69. **Unlocking the Secrets of the Dashopanishads**
70. A Cultural Mosaic
71. Ancient Traditions, Modern Minds
72. Ecos of Ancient Wisdom
73. Beneath the Surface
74. From Temples to Ashrams
75. Sages of the Subcontinent
76. The Art of Healling (Ayurveda, Yoga & Naturopathy)
77. Indian Kitchen
78. The Festivals of India
79. The Indian Epics Retold
80. The Power of Mantras
81. The Indian River Ganges
82. The Indian Architecture
83. Rites of Passage
84. The Indian Silk Road
85. The Indian Literature
86. The Indian Villages
87. The Indian Folks & Crafts
88. The Way of Buddha
89. The Ramayan of Tulsidas

90. Astrological Remedies
91. The Secret Power of Motivation
92. Secret of Developing your Inner Strength
93. The Secret Path to Motivation
94. The Art and Secret of Positive Thinking
95. The Secrets of Practicing Ethical Living
96. Indian Art and Painting
97. The Indian Herbalism
98. Bharatanatyam to Kathak
99. Exploring India's Astrological Remedies
100. The Indian Festival of Flowers
101. Indian Handicrafts
102. The Splashes of Joy – India's Colour Festival
103. The Indian Science of Astrology
104. The Indian Mythology
105. Path to Enlightenment
106. The Indian Spirituality for Children
107. Aromas of India
108. The Secrets of Healthy Relationships
109. Ancestral Ties
110. The Indian Street Food
111. Discovering America
112. The Indian Textile
113. Listening to Motivational Speeches
114. Taste of India
115. A Cultural Journey through Indian Nuptials
116. Motivational Quote for Change
117. Secret Strategies for Making Money
118. Secrets to Cultivate a Positive Mindset

Contact

DR. JAGADEESH PILLAI

PhD in Vedic Science

Four Times Guinness World Record Holder

Winner of Mahatma Gandhi Vishwa Shanti Puraskar and Global Peace Ambassador

Gemology, Astro & Vastu Consultant - Spiritual Counselor

Consultant for designing World Record Ideas

Efficient Tarot Card Reader

9839093003

myrichindia@gmail.com

drjagadeeshpillai@facebook

drjagadeeshpillai@instagram

jagadeeshpillai@youtube

www. JAGADEESHPILLAI.com

|| LOKAHA SAMASTHAHA SUKHINO BHAVANTU ||

Printed by Libri Plureos GmbH in Hamburg,
Germany